FAITH, HOPE AND CHARITY

by the same author

TOTAL ECLIPSE
THE PHILANTHROPIST
SAVAGES
TREATS
ABLE'S WILL: A PLAY FOR TELEVISION
TALES FROM HOLLYWOOD

adaptations
George Steiner's THE PORTAGE TO SAN CRISTOBAL OF A.H.
Choderlos de Laclos's LES LIAISONS DANGEREUSES

translations
Ödön von Horváth's TALES FROM THE VIENNA WOODS
Ödön von Horváth's DON JUAN COMES BACK FROM THE WAR
Ibsen's THE WILD DUCK
Molière's TARTUFFE
Ibsen's HEDDA GABLER and A DOLL'S HOUSE

screenplays
Choderlos de Laclos's DANGEROUS LIAISONS
Oswald Wynd's THE GINGER TREE

FAITH, HOPE AND CHARITY

a little dance of death in five acts

ÖDÖN VON HORVÁTH

Translated by
CHRISTOPHER HAMPTON

This play was written with the help
of Lucas Kristl

faber and faber
LONDON · BOSTON

First published in 1989
by Faber and Faber Limited
3 Queen Square London WC1N 3AU

Photoset by Wilmaset Birkenhead Wirral
Printed in Great Britain by
Richard Clay Ltd Bungay Suffolk

A CIP record for this book
is available from the British Library

ISBN 0-571-14106-4

For Ian

Passing through Munich in February 1932, I came across an acquaintance called Lukas Kristl, who for some years has been a court reporter. He spoke to me more or less as follows: I (Kristl) don't understand why playwrights, when they make a dramatic adaptation of the circumstances and consequences of a crime, almost always pick on so-called capital crimes, which are relatively rarely committed and hardly ever bother with minor crimes of the sort you encounter by the thousand the length and breadth of the country, the circumstances of which are as often as not shrouded in ignorance, but the consequences of which, in terms of loss of civil rights, nevertheless equally often resemble those following a life sentence or even a death sentence.

And Kristl told me about a case he had come across – and this everyday case was the origin of the little dance of death *Faith, Hope and Charity*. The characters of Elisabeth, the policeman (Alfons Klostermeyer), the magistrate's wife and the chief inspector, Kristl knew personally. So I need to thank him here for making available his raw material and for a great deal of stimulation.

Kristl's intention was to write a play against the irresponsibly bureaucratic application of minor regulations – naturally in the knowledge that there will always be minor regulations, because there must be in any community however constituted. So in the end Kristl's intention was to articulate the hope that these minor regulations might (if you'll forgive a harsh expression) perhaps be more humanely applied.

Which was also my intention, or certainly I was clear in my mind that this anti-minor regulations theme would undoubtedly provide the material to be able to portray once again the gigantic struggle between the individual and society, this eternal battle with no peaceful outcome – during which the individual can at best enjoy for a few moments the illusion of a ceasefire.

As with all my plays, I have made a great effort with this little dance of death not to forget that this, the individual's hopeless struggle, is fuelled by animal instinct and that therefore the problem of whether this struggle is pursued by heroic or cowardly means may be considered merely as a formal aspect of animality, which as we know is neither good nor evil.

As in all my plays I have on this occasion neither prettified nor disfigured. Whoever makes a conscientious attempt to characterize us human beings must undoubtedly acknowledge (unless his grasp of human nature is slight) that our expressions of feeling are tainted with kitsch, that is to say falsified, euphemistic, masochistically lusting for sympathy, no doubt as a result of a lazy-minded need to be accepted – and so whoever tries to characterize human beings honestly will always be confined to building mirrors, and here I would like to take the opportunity briefly to emphasize the following: I have never built and will never build distorting mirrors, because I reject parody in all its forms.

As in all my plays I have also tried on this occasion to be as disrespectful as possible towards stupidity and lies, on the grounds that this disrespectfulness might well represent the principal duty of a literary artist who sometimes imagines his only motive for writing is to allow people to recognize themselves. Please recognize yourself! So that you may acquire that cheerfulness which will alleviate your own life-and-death struggle by virtue of the fact that a dose of honesty places you certainly not above yourself (for that would be conceited) but next to and below yourself, so that in spite of everything you are able to contemplate yourself not from on high, but from in front, behind, sideways and from underneath!

Any one of my plays could be called 'Faith, Hope and Charity'. And the following passage from the Bible could stand as epigraph to any one of my plays:

And the LORD smelled a sweet savour; and the LORD said in his heart, I will not again curse the ground any more for man's sake; for the imagination of man's heart *is* evil from his youth; neither will I again smite any more every thing living, as I have done.

While the earth remaineth, seedtime and harvest, and cold and heat, and summer and winter, and day and night shall not cease.

Genesis, 8, xxi–xxii

ÖDÖN VON HORVÁTH

TRANSLATOR'S NOTE

Faith, Hope and Charity is pared down and chiselled from a mass of frequently fascinating material eventually rejected by Horváth. I have, with one exception, respected this impressive self-discipline. Among the papers relating to the play is a single sheet headed 'Monolog der Elisabeth'. In Heribert Sasse's Berlin production this speech, delivered by the actress as she moved through the auditorium, opened the play. In the summer of 1989, the Horváth archive came up for sale at Sotheby's (where it failed to make its reserve) and I was able to find the sheet of paper in question. Scrawled on it in red crayon was the indication that the speech was intended for Act Two. This may refer to an Act Two from an earlier draft (scenes in the zoo, back at Elisabeth's home and next to a sports car on the side of a country road were all, in various drafts, known as Act Two), but the speech (which begins 'It's nearly eight months . . .' on page 16 and ends '. . . the best way to get a job.') seemed to me to sit very well at the end of the present Act Two. I have omitted one or two phrases (including, for example, a reference to a character no longer in the play) and changed some tenses to fit the context; otherwise the whole speech has been translated. Purists may omit it: but I feel that apart from being touching and beautifully written, it provides, at a distance of fifty years, valuable background which a contemporary audience might not have found necessary. Perhaps Horváth was afraid it might seem self-pitying: Heribert and I decided the risk was worth taking.

I should like, once again, to thank Ian Huish for his invaluable help and advice.

C.H.

CHARACTERS

ELISABETH
A POLICEMAN (ALFONS KLOSTERMEYER)
CHIEF DISSECTOR
DISSECTOR
ASSISTANT DISSECTOR
THE BARON IN MOURNING
IRENE PRANTL
THE MAGISTRATE'S WIFE
HIMSELF, THE MAGISTRATE
A DISABLED VETERAN
A WORKER'S WIFE
A BOOK-KEEPER
MARIA
A DETECTIVE
THE CHIEF INSPECTOR
SECOND POLICEMAN
THIRD POLICEMAN
JOACHIM, THE DARING YOUNG LIFESAVER

Faith, Hope and Charity was first performed on 27 October 1989 at the Lyric Theatre, Hammersmith. The play was directed by Heribert Sasse and designed by Santiago del Corral.

ACT ONE

SCENE ONE

The setting: in front of the Anatomical Institute, with its frosted-glass windows. ELISABETH *wants to go in and is looking around questioningly, but there's not a soul to be seen.*
In the distance a band intones Chopin's much-loved Funeral March, and now a young POLICEMAN (*Alfons Klostermeyer*) *strolls slowly past* ELISABETH, *apparently scarcely noticing her.*
It's springtime.

SCENE TWO

ELISABETH *speaks to the* POLICEMAN *all of a sudden, as the sound of the Funeral March fades into the distance.*

ELISABETH: Excuse me . . . it's just I'm looking for the Anatomy.
POLICEMAN: The Anatomical Institute?
ELISABETH: Where they cut up the corpses.
POLICEMAN: This is it, that there.
ELISABETH: That's all right then.
    (*Silence.*)
POLICEMAN: (*Smiling*) You take care, miss . . . there's heads in there, stacked up in rows.
ELISABETH: I'm not afraid of dead bodies.
POLICEMAN: Me neither.
ELISABETH: It's been a long time since I've been frightened of anything.
POLICEMAN: Likewise . . .
    (*A light gesture of farewell and he's gone.*)

I

SCENE THREE

ELISABETH *watches the* POLICEMAN *go, her expression ironic . . .
then she plucks up courage and presses the bell of the Anatomical
Institute. We hear it ring, inside, and then the* DISSECTOR *appears
in his white coat. He stands in the doorway, staring at the
apparently indecisive* ELISABETH.

SCENE FOUR

DISSECTOR: What do you want?

ELISABETH: I'd like to see someone in authority.

DISSECTOR: In what connection?

ELISABETH: It's quite urgent.

DISSECTOR: Are we looking after a corpse for you? A loved one?

ELISABETH: It's not to do with a corpse, it's to do with me
personally.

DISSECTOR: Whatever do you mean?

ELISABETH: Are you in a position of authority here?

DISSECTOR: I'm the Dissector, you can rely on me.
(*Silence.*)

ELISABETH: The thing is, I was told quite particularly, you
could sell your body here . . . what I mean is, once I'm
dead, the people in there could do what they like with my
body in the cause of science . . . but in the meantime I get
the fee for it paid out. Right now.

DISSECTOR: New one on me.

ELISABETH: But I was told quite particularly.

DISSECTOR: Who by?

ELISABETH: Someone at work.

DISSECTOR: What's your job, then?

ELISABETH: I don't really have anything just at the moment.
It'll be worse before it's better. But I never let it get me
down.
(*Silence.*)

2

DISSECTOR: Selling your own corpse . . . what's the world
    coming to?
ELISABETH: Beggars can't be choosers.
DISSECTOR: Ludicrous idea . . .
    (*He takes a bag of birdseed out of his pocket and feeds the
    pigeons, which fly down from the roof of the Anatomical
    Institute . . . the pigeons know the* DISSECTOR *well and perch
    on his shoulder and eat out of his hand.*)

SCENE FIVE

Now the CHIEF DISSECTOR *shows a* BARON *with a black armband
out of the Anatomical Institute into the fresh air.*

CHIEF DISSECTOR: Soon be out of the way, Baron; and once
    again, my deepest sympathy.
BARON: Thank you, doctor. I blame myself, you know.
CHIEF DISSECTOR: But the Public Prosecutor's Inquiry
    established the absolute insubstantiality of every
    single charge raised against you. All of us are in God's
    hands.
BARON: All the same: I was at Verdun and in the battle of the
    Somme, but nothing's ever affected me as much as that
    accident yesterday. We'd only been married for three
    months and I was driving . . . round that blind corner. Just
    between Lechbruch and Steingaden. Good thing they
    released the corpse.
    (*Meanwhile, the* CHIEF DISSECTOR *has noticed the*
    DISSECTOR.)
CHIEF DISSECTOR: One moment, if you'd be so kind. (*He comes
    right up to the* DISSECTOR, *screaming at him.*) Are you
    feeding those pigeons again? What do you think you're
    doing? This isn't a pigsty! There are fingers and pharynxes
    lying about all over the place! There are those hearts to be
    finished off, both of them *and* the remains of that spleen, if
    you'd be so kind! God help us all, it's chaos in there!

3

DISSECTOR: But this young lady was wanting to sell us her corpse, you see . . .

CHIEF DISSECTOR: Her corpse? What, again?

(*Silence.*)

BARON: Extraordinary.

CHIEF DISSECTOR: God knows how many times we've had to deny that we buy dead people when they're alive, doesn't anyone ever listen to official announcements? They get some idea, the state's going to pay out something for their body . . . what makes them think they're that interesting? The state, they think the state should take care of everything.

BARON: A quite extraordinary view of the responsibilities of the state.

CHIEF DISSECTOR: Things are going to change any minute, Baron.

BARON: Let's hope so.

SCENE SIX

The ASSISTANT DISSECTOR *hurriedly emerges from the Anatomical Institute with the Chief Dissector's hat.*

ASSISTANT DISSECTOR: Telephone, sir.

CHIEF DISSECTOR: What, for me?

ASSISTANT DISSECTOR: It's something to do with the verdict in the Leopoldine Hackinger case. The woman from Brno. You're supposed to go and see the Professor at the clinic right away . . .

(*He hands him his hat.*)

CHIEF DISSECTOR: Right away!

(*He scrambles out of his white coat and hands it to the* ASSISTANT DISSECTOR, *who vanishes back into the Anatomical Institute: then turns to the* BARON.)

Excuse me, Baron. Some woman from the Sudetenland: the experts can't seem to work out what it is she's died of. Duty calls . . .

4

BARON: Well, of course.

CHIEF DISSECTOR: . . . and once again, my deepest sympathy.

BARON: Well, thank you.

CHIEF DISSECTOR: It's been a privilege.

> (*He exits right, moving fast.*)

BARON: Bye . . .

> (*He exits left, moving slowly; and once again, far in the distance, a few phrases from Chopin's Funeral March. The light gradually begins to fade, as it's already late afternoon.*)

SCENE SEVEN

The DISSECTOR *watches the* CHIEF DISSECTOR *leave.*

DISSECTOR: Not a nice man. Poor pigeons. You want my advice, miss: best thing you can do is go home and throw yourself out the window.

ELISABETH: Well, you are a help.

DISSECTOR: I'm trying to do you a favour. Who's going to buy a corpse? Nowadays?

ELISABETH: Tomorrow is another day.

DISSECTOR: Nothing changes.

ELISABETH: I don't believe that.

DISSECTOR: Oh, you don't?

> (*Silence.* ELISABETH *smiles.*)

ELISABETH: No . . . I'm not going to let you convince me my luck won't change. Listen, suppose I'd been able to sell my corpse for let's say a hundred and fifty marks . . .

DISSECTOR: (*Interrupting her*) A hundred and fifty marks?

ELISABETH: That's right.

> (*The* DISSECTOR *grins.*)

DISSECTOR: You're like a child . . .

ELISABETH: Why do you say that?

DISSECTOR: What's your father do?

ELISABETH: He's an inspector.

5

DISSECTOR: An inspector? Well well!

ELISABETH: But he can't support me just at the moment, because my mum passed away in March and he's had a lot of expense.

DISSECTOR: What's a humble chief dissector compared to an inspector? Well well, miss!

ELISABETH: See, if I had a hundred and fifty marks, I could get my sales permit and then there's no knowing what I could do . . . because with my sales permit I could start tomorrow, I could find a more or less self-supporting job in my original line I got thrown out of because of the Depression.

(*Silence.*)

DISSECTOR: What sort of line was that, then?

ELISABETH: Girdles, corsetry. Wholesale. And bras, all that sort of thing.

DISSECTOR: Interesting.

(*Silence.*)

ELISABETH: Where is the life that once I knew?

(*Silence. The* DISSECTOR *fumbles with his wallet and fetches out a photograph.*)

DISSECTOR: Have a look at this . . .

(ELISABETH *contemplates the photograph.*)

ELISABETH: Nice dog.

DISSECTOR: Little terrier . . .

ELISABETH: Intelligent looking.

DISSECTOR: And snappy! Unfortunately, he handed in his dinner pail.

ELISABETH: Shame.

(*The* DISSECTOR *whistles.*)

DISSECTOR: That was his whistle. He'd always come. (*He addresses the photograph.*) Good boy, you're gone now, aren't you, my good boy . . . no more walkies . . . (*He puts the photograph away and turns to* ELISABETH.) It's really nice of you to be so sympathetic about my poor old chap. What's your Christian name?

ELISABETH: Elisabeth.

(*Silence.*)

DISSECTOR: Empress Elisabeth of Austria, there's another
gallant little woman . . . didn't stop terrorists picking her
off. In Geneva. Where the League of Nations is . . . and
that's another racket! I still have my butterfly collection
and a canary; and a cat made friends with me yesterday.
Are you interested in aquaria?

ELISABETH: What?

DISSECTOR: I've got a terrarium as well.

ELISABETH: Terrarium sounds even better.

DISSECTOR: Well, then you must come and pay me a visit.

ELISABETH: Maybe.

SCENE EIGHT

Now the CHIEF DISSECTOR, *on his way back from the clinic,*
makes a somewhat surprising entrance: his finger is thickly
bandaged. He observes the DISSECTOR, *stopping indignantly and*
staring at him, as he makes to move away, while ELISABETH *also*
withdraws.

SCENE NINE

The CHIEF DISSECTOR *slowly approaches the* DISSECTOR *and stops*
right in front of him.

CHIEF DISSECTOR: What again? Are you still feeding those
pigeons? (*He suddenly lets fly at him.*) Will you make
yourself scarce! (*He turns to* ELISABETH.) Is that
understood?

ELISABETH: Yes.
(*She goes.*)

7

SCENE TEN

The CHIEF DISSECTOR *watches* ELISABETH *leave.*

CHIEF DISSECTOR: Well, this is just what the doctor ordered. I thought you might be cataloguing those tumours at last, not standing around entertaining the weaker sex.

DISSECTOR: That's where you're wrong. Her father is a government inspector fallen on hard times.

CHIEF DISSECTOR: A government inspector?

DISSECTOR: That's right. And if she could get a hundred and fifty marks, she'd have her sales permit and there's no knowing what she could do . . . I know you think I'm incompetent, just because I have an aquarium and I feed the pigeons and I'm kind-hearted . . .

CHIEF DISSECTOR: Get to the point.

DISSECTOR: The point is I'm going to take this government inspector's daughter under my wing and support her. I've made up my mind. A hundred and fifty marks.

CHIEF DISSECTOR: A hundred and fifty?

DISSECTOR: She'll pay me back.

CHIEF DISSECTOR: I think you're an impulsive party who still believes in miracles. If you were my wife, I'd beat your head in . . .
  (He threatens him roguishly with his thickly bandaged finger.)

DISSECTOR: What's wrong with your finger? Hurt yourself?

CHIEF DISSECTOR: An infection.

DISSECTOR: Not from a corpse?

CHIEF DISSECTOR: Where else? Just now. That tricky case from Brno.

DISSECTOR: You want to be careful of that, sir.
  (Silence. The CHIEF DISSECTOR *considers his thickly bandaged finger.)*

CHIEF DISSECTOR: It doesn't hurt; that's funny . . .

DISSECTOR: Whenever I consider my butterfly collection, for

8

example, I always think everything is organized according to some higher plan.

CHIEF DISSECTOR: You're rambling again: come along, duty calls!

(*He exits with the* DISSECTOR *into the Anatomical Institute. Darkness.*)

ACT TWO

SCENE ONE

The setting: the office in Irene Prantl's shop. IRENE PRANTL *is a garrulous woman, particularly in her professional life. At the moment she's at her desk, busy with her accounts, looking very important. In front of her sits a* MAGISTRATE'S WIFE. *In the background, wax dummies wearing corsets, girdles, brassières and so on . . . stacked up in rows, like the heads in the Anatomical Institute.*

PRANTL: I really have to take my hat off to you! Seven girdles, six corsets and eleven pairs of suspenders in three days flat . . . congratulations! You've got the knack! Better than most of the professionals! Real talent!

MAGISTRATE'S WIFE: Well, goodness, as a magistrate's wife, I move in certain social circles, acquaintances, you know, who scarcely want to be seen turning me down . . .

PRANTL: No, you're too modest! It's not a piece of cake these days, selling, people slam the door in your face!

MAGISTRATE'S WIFE: But I must insist on our agreement: if anyone asks, naturally you'll say I'm only selling these things as a sort of hobby . . .

PRANTL: Goes without saying, it'll be our secret!

MAGISTRATE'S WIFE: Times are hard when you have to support your own husband, *and* he's earning over six hundred marks. People are being laid off left, right and centre, not the county-court judges of course or the top civil servants . . .

(*She breaks off as the telephone rings.* PRANTL *answers it.*)

PRANTL: Yes. Send her in . . . one second, if you don't mind, this won't take a minute.

SCENE TWO

ELISABETH *enters.*

PRANTL: Good morning, come in, let's have a look . . . Where's
　　your book of words?
ELISABETH: Here . . .
　　(*She hands over her order book.* PRANTL *leafs through it.*)
PRANTL: What? Two pairs of suspenders, a girdle and a corset,
　　you might as well not bother!
ELISABETH: It's not a piece of cake these days, selling, people
　　slam the door in your face.
PRANTL: No need to be vulgar! Your job as a saleswoman is to
　　develop the customer's feeling for beauty! The whole
　　country's exercise-mad now, you see naked women
　　everywhere, what could be better publicity for our lines?
　　And you've got to pay more attention to our lords and
　　masters, I've never met a man yet who wasn't interested in
　　suspender belts! How did you do in Kaufbeuren?
ELISABETH: I didn't do anything in Kaufbeuren.
PRANTL: What do you mean? Kaufbeuren's always been
　　astronomical!
ELISABETH: But I didn't get to Kaufbeuren.
PRANTL: Why not?
ELISABETH: I wanted to save time, so I got a lift, straight there
　　as the crow flies . . . but all of a sudden the car broke down
　　and I had to spend the night in a barn in the forest.
　　(PRANTL *lets fly at her.*)
PRANTL: In the forest? What do you think I'm paying you for?
　　If that's the way the crow flies, it'll be Judgement Day
　　before you work off that hundred and fifty marks I
　　advanced you for your sales permit!
ELISABETH: It was an act of God.
PRANTL: When my employees start in with acts of God, it's all
　　over as far as I'm concerned! That's when I cut my throat!
　　Blood-poisoning or falling out of the train and breaking

12

a leg, that I can just about wear, but Irene Prantl
has never yet surrendered to the luxury of an act of
God!

ELISABETH: There's nothing I can do about it.

PRANTL: And don't look so pained, little Miss Act of God! Just
look at this lady! She's married to a magistrate, she doesn't
need a job, it's purely a hobby and she's done four times
your turnover.

SCENE THREE

The DISSECTOR *bursts in and immediately lets fly at* ELISABETH.
He's beside himself.

DISSECTOR: There you are, you impostor! You swindler! Your
father's not a government inspector. He's just some claims
inspector in an insurance office. If you hadn't told me he
was a government inspector, do you think I'd have
provided for you like that?

ELISABETH: I never said anything of the sort . . .

DISSECTOR: (*Interrupting her*) Yes, you did, that's exactly what
you said!

ELISABETH: No! Never!
(*The* DISSECTOR *smashes his walking stick down on Prantl's
desk, scattering papers and bellowing.*)

DISSECTOR: Government inspector! You said government
inspector!
(PRANTL *rescues her papers, shrieking.*)

PRANTL: Stop it!
(*Silence. The* DISSECTOR *bows chivalrously to* PRANTL *and
the* MAGISTRATE'S WIFE.)

DISSECTOR: Do excuse me, ladies, out of a clear blue sky,
but compared to a claims inspector, even a humble
chief dissector is a person of some authority and
this dangerous woman has inveigled good money out of
me . . .

13

ELISABETH: (*Interrupting him*) It's just not true!

PRANTL: Be quiet!

DISSECTOR: Be quiet!

(PRANTL *waves a threatening finger*.)

PRANTL: Now, now, miss . . . a raised voice is a sure sign of guilt.

DISSECTOR: (*Raising his voice*) Guilt! That's right!

(*Silence*.)

ELISABETH: I won't say another word.

DISSECTOR: (*Malevolently*) That'd just suit you, wouldn't it?

PRANTL: (*To the* DISSECTOR) Please sit down.

DISSECTOR: Thank you . . . (*He sits down*.) I'm a very kind-hearted man, but I will not tolerate being lied to.

ELISABETH: I never lied to you.

PRANTL: Will you stop interrupting . . .

DISSECTOR: Yes, thank you.

(PRANTL *offers the* DISSECTOR *a cigarette*.)

PRANTL: Do you?

DISSECTOR: Yes, I'll take the liberty . . . (*He lights up, settles himself comfortably, exhaling voluptuously*.) So, ladies . . . she comes to my flat, she takes advantage of my paternal instincts, I show her my aquarium and lend her my book on Tibet and over and above all that I pay for her sales permit . . . and all the time her father isn't a government inspector! I made inquiries, just to put my mind at rest, because my colleagues are always making fun of my soft-heartedness.

PRANTL: Sales permit? What sales permit? She got that from me.

DISSECTOR: What? You as well?

PRANTL: It's company policy. The firm offers it to employees in the form of an optional advance which they can work off. A hundred and fifty marks.

DISSECTOR: (*Beside himself*) A hundred and fifty marks?

PRANTL: That's fraud.

(ELISABETH *suddenly lets fly*.)

ELISABETH: I am not a criminal!

14

MAGISTRATE'S WIFE: That's not what matters, miss, your opinion. Whether there's material evidence of fraud, that's what matters. Otherwise justice would grind to a halt.

PRANTL: Quite right.

MAGISTRATE'S WIFE: It's none of my business and personally I thank God I have nothing to do with the law except that I happen to be married to a judge. But if you didn't use this gentleman's money to buy your sales permit, then . . . my August would say, I can hear him now: misrepresentation of the facts . . . material evidence of fraud.
(*The* DISSECTOR *has slumped despairingly.*)

DISSECTOR: (*Lachrymose*) I'm only a poor dissector who tried to do a good deed . . .

ELISABETH: You'll get your money back.

DISSECTOR: No.

ELISABETH: Yes, you will, every penny.

DISSECTOR: When?

ELISABETH: I'll work it off.

PRANTL: Oh? How? (*She reads from Elisabeth's order book.*) Two pairs of suspenders, a girdle and a corset. And an act of God.

DISSECTOR: (*Exploding*) 'Act of God'? Fraud! Give me my money back this minute!

ELISABETH: I haven't got it.

PRANTL: But I gave you your sales permit.

ELISABETH: That's true.

DISSECTOR: Well, then!

ELISABETH: I needed the money this man lent me for something more urgent.

PRANTL: Curiouser and curiouser!

ELISABETH: It was personal. I needed it to pay a fine.
(*The* DISSECTOR *is beside himself again.*)

DISSECTOR: What? You've already had a brush with the law? You've got a previous conviction? I'll put you in gaol for this, I promise you that! I was your last victim!
(*He storms out.*)

15

PRANTL: Wonderful! That's wonderful!

MAGISTRATE'S WIFE: If that gentleman testifies under oath about the government inspector and the claims inspector, they'll find you guilty.

PRANTL: Gaol.

MAGISTRATE'S WIFE: But don't worry. Only prison, that's all. And not more than fourteen days.

ELISABETH: Everyone'll think I'm some arch-criminal.

PRANTL: You can't stop people thinking, especially seeing as you kept quiet about your previous conviction.

ELISABETH: I'm under no obligation to tell you anything.

PRANTL: Don't be so superior! This scandal is a disgrace. Naturally you're dismissed at once . . . but now you wait here, while I fetch the police.
(*She exits.*)

SCENE FIVE

MAGISTRATE'S WIFE: It's none of my business, but a previous conviction always looks bad.

(ELISABETH *recites her answer like a schoolgirl.*)

ELISABETH: I have a previous conviction because I once worked without a sales permit . . . so they slapped a hundred and fifty mark fine on me, payable in instalments. But eventually it all came due and I would have had to go to prison and I'd have gone under . . . so I used the dissector's money to pay my fine. It's nearly eight months since I was made redundant . . . and I had to clear out of my room and pawn my brooch . . . I tried sharing with a friend, we didn't get on but I never let it get me down. So I went on my travels and they said things were getting better and there'd be jobs again, otherwise there'd be riots and revolution. Except I couldn't find a job and there was no revolution, but I never let it get me down. And people stayed calm and kept their mouths shut, or if they didn't, they were locked up . . . and when I looked at the Situations Wanted in the paper my stomach turned over, but I never let it get me down. And in the paper it talked about the misery of the people and the Minister said the state is a welfare state and that that was the whole trouble. Undermined morale and killed initiative and so on and so forth. And I found out how difficult it was to get on with other people. But I never let it get me down. And you were cheated and exploited everywhere, at least you were if you had nothing. So I said to the state: 'Listen, I'm a citizen too,' but the state didn't answer. And then I found this job, but to get it I needed money. A genuine job as a saleswoman . . . and I needed a deposit of a hundred and fifty marks. Well, I wasn't going to let that get me down! I still believe my luck is bound to change . . . it's the only faith I have left. And faith moves mountains and I'm not going to let anything get me down. I spent my last bit of money on make-up: it's still the best way to get a job. (*Silence.*)

MAGISTRATE'S WIFE: All you have to remember is don't keep denying everything and don't pretend to be cleverer than the judge. My husband's a good man, but don't let the defence drag the case out just for the sake of it. If I'm sitting at home with his lunch waiting for him and he can't get away because the sitting's going on so long, that's when he starts to get unreasonable . . . You see, the accused needs to have some consideration as well, after all, a judge is only human.
(*Darkness.*)

ACT THREE

SCENE ONE

The setting: in front of the Social Security Office with its minimal front garden.
A group of clients of the Social Security Office are having a discussion; a WORKER'S WIFE, *an elderly* BOOK-KEEPER *and a young woman called* MARIA. ELISABETH *is there too. She's leaning against the garden railings, catching some watery late afternoon sun. Now, a disabled* VETERAN *hobbles out of the Social Security Office.*

SCENE TWO

VETERAN: Well, three cheers! Now the Social Security turn round and say it's not their responsibility, I'm supposed to be somewhere else . . . Bloody hell!

WORKER'S WIFE: You'll be wanting the Pensions Office.

VETERAN: Pensions Office says, it's nothing to do with them, it's a National Insurance matter. Insurance says, my feet was already done in before the accident, because of my varicose veins and fallen arches . . . and their tame expert says to my face I could've been walking about without a stick for years if I put my mind to it!

BOOK-KEEPER: Have you tried the Appeals Tribunal?

VETERAN: All they did was agreed the National Insurance could cut my money down from 60 per cent to 40 . . . they stuck an extra paragraph on my arbitration, saying the plaintiff had no incentive to look for a job, because when he was working, he was not earning significantly more than he is from his pension!

SCENE THREE

Now everyone falls silent and remains motionless, while a
POLICEMAN *(Alfons Klostermeyer) strolls slowly by, apparently
taking no notice of anyone. Already the light is gradually beginning
to fade.*

SCENE FOUR

The WORKER'S WIFE *watches the* POLICEMAN *leave.*

WORKER'S WIFE: There goes the general . . .

BOOK-KEEPER: Give us this day our daily bread.

MARIA: My problem's even worse.

VETERAN: How come?

MARIA: There's seven in my family and the eighth is on the way
. . . but because my father's bringing home forty marks a
week, they've started making stoppages.

VETERAN: It's all a racket.

ELISABETH: They wouldn't give me anything, because my
father's still earning.

BOOK-KEEPER: What's he do, your father?

ELISABETH: Claims inspector in an insurance office. I'm sorry, I
have to laugh . . .
(*She laughs.*)

WORKER'S WIFE: What are you laughing at, you silly cow?
(ELISABETH *stops laughing abruptly.*)
All you have to do is go home.

ELISABETH: No!

WORKER'S WIFE: Then it's your own fault. If your father's an
inspector . . .

ELISABETH: (*Interrupting her*) Claims inspector in an insurance
office!

WORKER'S WIFE: Same difference!

ELISABETH: (*Grinning*) Is it?

20

BOOK-KEEPER: A fool and his pride are never parted.
WORKER'S WIFE: A home to go to and won't take advantage!
ELISABETH: There's good reason for it.
WORKER'S WIFE: Have you done something wrong?
    (ELISABETH *smiles uncertainly*.)
ELISABETH: Does it show?
    (*Silence. The* BOOK-KEEPER *grins*.)
BOOK-KEEPER: All that glisters is not gold . . .
    (*He exits*.)

SCENE FIVE

MARIA: (*To* ELISABETH) You just have to learn to put up with
    it.
ELISABETH: I don't want to talk about it.

SCENE SIX

The VETERAN *counts on his fingers, talking to himself*.

VETERAN: Social Security Office. Job Centre. National
    Insurance. Pensions Office. Appeals Tribunal . . . see you
    in the mass grave!
    (*He exits*.)

SCENE SEVEN

WORKER'S WIFE: (*To herself*) The mass grave . . . that's how
    long you have to wait before they take care of you.
    (*She exits*.)

MARIA: What you do wrong?

ELISABETH: Nothing.

MARIA: Did they lock you up?

(ELISABETH *doesn't answer.*)

Don't worry, you can tell me . . . I know how it goes. It's only some pissy little rule, but you get caught . . . You don't really know what you've done, but it's all over. Listen, they threw my father inside for ten days because he brought home a couple of planks from the building site . . . they were just lying around and our roof was leaking, rain coming in on the beds. If you do something wrong, you'd better be sure it's really worthwhile.

(ELISABETH *still doesn't answer. It's dark now and the two women are alone, perching on the base of the railings, lit by the light streaming out of the windows of the Social Security Office.*)

Ever been married?

ELISABETH: No.

(*Silence.*)

See, my father and I are different sorts of people. I mean, when I was born, he was furious I was only a girl. And he went on holding it against me. On the other hand he makes out he's a man of the world. If my mother was alive, she could tell you a few sad stories. Men are all selfish bastards.

MARIA: You just haven't found the right one.

ELISABETH: Maybe.

MARIA: He'll come out of the blue. Just when you least expect it.

(*Silence.*)

ELISABETH: I like one man in every ten thousand, at the most.

MARIA: Well, yes.

ELISABETH: I've always wanted to be independent . . . you know, my own master.

MARIA: Never works.
  (*Silence.*)
  I got nothing against getting married. Long as he didn't
  beat me . . . What you doing now?
ELISABETH: Nothing.
  (*Silence.*)
MARIA: You can call me Maria.
ELISABETH: All right.
  (*Silence. Suddenly* MARIA *gets up.*)
MARIA: Come on! Let's see what we can do . . . there's a bloke
  over there, he'll buy us a ham roll.
ELISABETH: No, I don't want to.
  (*Silence.*)
MARIA: Why not?
ELISABETH: No. Self-preservation.
  (*Silence.*)
MARIA: Pull the other one, it's got bells on . . .

SCENE NINE

Now the BARON *with the black armband appears . . . he looks
somewhat battered, tired and embittered.* MARIA *catches sight of him
and stares at him, fascinated.*

SCENE TEN

The BARON *bows gallantly.*

BARON: Good evening, my dear. I was afraid you might not put
  in an appearance.
MARIA: (*Tonelessly*) I said I would.
  (*Silence. The* BARON *recognizes* ELISABETH.)
BARON: Ah!
  (*He raises his hat and smiles maliciously.*)
MARIA: Oh? You know my friend from out of town?

23

BARON: Out of town? (*To* ELISABETH) You're the one who
wanted to sell your valuable corpse, aren't you?
MARIA: Corpse?
(*The* BARON *slides off his somewhat crumpled armband.*)
BARON: Yes, those were the days. I had my own business
then . . .
(ELISABETH *grins.*)
ELISABETH: Corsets, was it?
BARON: No, liquor. Now I'm broke.
(MARIA *is looking at herself in her hand mirror, in the light
from the Social Security Office.*)
MARIA: Hugo! Notice anything different?
BARON: I can't quite put my finger on it.
MARIA: There . . . (*She shows her teeth.*) I had them crowned the
day before yesterday, these two front ones . . . see, these
two used to be all black and broken down, the nerves were
dead.
(*The* BARON *smiles cunningly.*)
BARON: You've improved your prospects.
MARIA: Pleased to hear it.

SCENE ELEVEN

Now a DETECTIVE *appears, behind* MARIA, *who is still inspecting
her crowns in the hand mirror. The* BARON *withdraws somewhat
and the* DETECTIVE *waits until* MARIA *turns round. Now she
notices him and starts.*

SCENE TWELVE

DETECTIVE: You come with me. You know why.
MARIA: (*Subdued*) No, I don't.
DETECTIVE: Oh, so you don't . . .
BARON: Where are my cufflinks?
(*Silence.*)

24

MARIA: (*Quietly*) Jesus Christ.
BARON: Who do you think stole them?
DETECTIVE: I'm a police officer. Come with me.
    (MARIA *stares at the* BARON.)
MARIA: You turned me in.
DETECTIVE: You keep your mouth shut.
MARIA: You did. And I lent you three marks. Three marks!
DETECTIVE: Shut up.
    (*Another gallant bow from the* BARON.)
BARON: Good evening, my dear.
    (*He exits.*)
MARIA: You pig, you shit!
    (*The* DETECTIVE *swiftly handcuffs her.*)
DETECTIVE: Shut up! Move!
    (*He drags her off.*)
MARIA: Ow!

SCENE THIRTEEN

The POLICEMAN (*Alfons Klostermeyer*) *hurries up towards the sound of the disturbance, stops and looks at* ELISABETH.

SCENE FOURTEEN

POLICEMAN: What's all this, then?
    (ELISABETH *smiles maliciously.*)
ELISABETH: Nothing. Just a woman being arrested. For no reason.
POLICEMAN: No, they wouldn't do that.
ELISABETH: All the same.
    (*Silence.*)
    Why are you staring at me?
POLICEMAN: (*Smiling*) Is there a law against it?
    (*Silence.*)
    The thing is you remind me of someone. Your general

demeanour. One of the dear departed.

ELISABETH: You're very mysterious.

(*Silence.*)

POLICEMAN: Which way are you going?

ELISABETH: Do you want to walk me home?

POLICEMAN: I'm off duty.

ELISABETH: I'd rather go on my own.

POLICEMAN: (*With no ulterior motive*) Don't you like the police?

ELISABETH: (*Starting somewhat*) Why do you say that?

POLICEMAN: Because you don't want me to walk you home.
There have to be police, miss! I mean, deep in every one of
us there's a mass murderer.

ELISABETH: Not in me.

POLICEMAN: Go on, there's no such thing!

ELISABETH: (*Imitating him*) 'There's no such thing!'

POLICEMAN: (*Smiling*) You're behaving like someone that's
been condemned to death.

ELISABETH: Not that anyone would give a damn.

POLICEMAN: Hope springs eternal.

ELISABETH: That's just a saying.

(*Silence.*)

POLICEMAN: Without faith, hope and charity, how could life go
on? It all connects logically.

ELISABETH: It's all very well for you to say that, you're an
official, your position is secure.

POLICEMAN: We all have to die.

ELISABETH: Don't talk to me about charity!

(*Silence.*)

POLICEMAN: Listen, miss. Just listen to me for a minute . . .
I've been watching you here in front of the Social Security
Office for days now. Because you remind me of someone
. . . like I said, one of the dear departed.

ELISABETH: Who was this dear departed?

POLICEMAN: My fiancée.

(*Silence.*)

We were like this. But she had something up with her liver
and now I really miss her. What's so funny?

26

ELISABETH: Nothing.
    (*Silence.*)
POLICEMAN: You seem very bitter.
ELISABETH: I'm a fast walker.
POLICEMAN: You walk as fast as you like, I'll keep up with you.
    (*A shot rings out in the distance . . . then another and another;
    somebody cries out. Silence. The* POLICEMAN *listens.*)
    What was that? Sounds as if they're shooting at
    each other again. There'll be civil war soon, it's just
    insanity . . . I'll just go and have a look, be right back,
    wait for me.
ELISABETH: All right.
    (*The* POLICEMAN *exits right.*)

SCENE FIFTEEN

Now the MAGISTRATE'S WIFE *and himself, the* MAGISTRATE,
enter left.

MAGISTRATE'S WIFE: This way, August! And in you go to the
    Social Security Office and tell the Privy Counsellor you're
    afraid you can't be at his disposal this evening, because
    you're promised to your better half.
MAGISTRATE: But you know I don't like going to the cinema.
    No cigars for two hours.
MAGISTRATE'S WIFE: Does you good! Remember your
    bowels!
MAGISTRATE: I know. The doctor warned me about them only
    yesterday.
MAGISTRATE'S WIFE: He warned me as well, he told me I
    shouldn't climb steps with my glands . . .
MAGISTRATE: (*Interrupting her*) Then why do you have to sell
    corsets? Complete lunacy!
MAGISTRATE'S WIFE: I don't want to have to come crawling on
    my knees for every penny!
MAGISTRATE: It's wrong to exaggerate! What do you know

27

about real poverty? You don't have to sentence poor people day in and day out, whose only real crime is not having a roof over their head.

MAGISTRATE'S WIFE: In that case, I wouldn't sentence them.

MAGISTRATE: Hermine!

(*Silence.*)

So. Now I have to tell the Privy Counsellor that our cribbage game is up the spout, because I'm promised to my better half . . . but if your film's another dud, you'd better watch out, Mickey Mouse . . .

(*He exits into the Social Security Office.*)

SCENE SIXTEEN

Now the MAGISTRATE'S WIFE *looks at* ELISABETH. *They stare at each other, but* ELISABETH *no longer wants to know anyone from her past . . . however, the* MAGISTRATE'S WIFE *won't give way.*

SCENE SEVENTEEN

MAGISTRATE'S WIFE: Funny. We've met . . .

(ELISABETH *looks around, frightened.*)

ELISABETH: Please don't recognize me . . .

MAGISTRATE'S WIFE: Don't be afraid! It's none of my business, but how long did you get?

ELISABETH: Fourteen days.

MAGISTRATE'S WIFE: See, that's exactly what I told you.

ELISABETH: And no remission.

MAGISTRATE'S WIFE: No?

ELISABETH: Because I had a previous conviction when they fined me . . . (*She grins.*) If I knew what I'd done wrong . . .

MAGISTRATE'S WIFE: Yes, I know how it happens! You don't have to tell me! Plain injustice . . . and I suppose you haven't been able to find a new job?

28

ELISABETH: No. But I met a man just now and he told me
about the death of his fiancée . . .
(*She grins again.*)
MAGISTRATE'S WIFE: No question it'd be the best thing for
you: marriage.
ELISABETH: (*Tonelessly*) I wouldn't say no.
MAGISTRATE'S WIFE: Well, congratulations.
ELISABETH: We met purely by chance.
MAGISTRATE'S WIFE: Always the same. And I know. I know!
ELISABETH: Maybe it's my big chance.
MAGISTRATE'S WIFE: What's he do, your intended?
ELISABETH: He's an official.
MAGISTRATE'S WIFE: An official? Does he know about the
fourteen days?
ELISABETH: No.
MAGISTRATE'S WIFE: Ah. Well, you must tell him, otherwise it
might eventually cause him difficulties in his career . . .
ELISABETH: Is that possible?
MAGISTRATE'S WIFE: Absolutely.
ELISABETH: There he is, he's coming back.
MAGISTRATE'S WIFE: Where? . . . What, a policeman? . . .
Well, it's nothing to do with me. Good luck.
(*She moves away from her.*)

SCENE EIGHTEEN

The POLICEMAN *reappears, speaks to* ELISABETH.

POLICEMAN: Well, I'm free now. Some passer-by got shot. Why
should we have to live in times like these, that's what I
often think . . . (*Suddenly, he points at the* MAGISTRATE'S
WIFE.) That woman, what'd she want?
ELISABETH: (*Lying*) I don't know her.
POLICEMAN: It's just she's staring at us.
ELISABETH: Perhaps she's mixing us up. It's easy to mix people
up.

POLICEMAN: That's true. On the other hand, if I as a representative of state authority were to mix two people up . . . well, it wouldn't be good for my career.

ELISABETH: Are they really that strict?

POLICEMAN: Very. And often it's completely unjust. Are you cold, is that why your teeth are chattering?

ELISABETH: Yes.

POLICEMAN: Very?

ELISABETH: Quite.

POLICEMAN: I'd happily give you my coat, I certainly don't need it, but it's not allowed.

ELISABETH: (*Smiling*) Your coat's still on duty.

POLICEMAN: Rules are rules.

ELISABETH: Come on, the wind's wicked . . .
      (*She exits slowly with the* POLICEMAN.)

SCENE NINETEEN

Now the MAGISTRATE *emerges from the Social Security Office. His* WIFE's *tone is quite gossipy, all of a sudden.*

MAGISTRATE'S WIFE: Listen, August . . . that's that girl from Prantl's over there, you know, that case of fraud about the claims inspector and the government inspector.

MAGISTRATE: I don't know what you're talking about.

MAGISTRATE'S WIFE: But you sentenced her . . .

MAGISTRATE: It's quite possible.
      (*Silence.*)

MAGISTRATE'S WIFE: You should have given her some remission, though, I don't call that very just . . .

MAGISTRATE: (*Furious*) You worry about your own injustices, Hermine!
      (*Darkness.*)

ACT FOUR

SCENE ONE

The setting: Elisabeth's bed-sitting room.
The POLICEMAN *(Alfons Klostermeyer) lies in bed in his*
underpants, dozing. ELISABETH *is brewing coffee, glancing from*
time to time at the white autumn asters which stand in a vase next to
the Primus stove.
Outside, the October sun shines, but the curtains are half drawn and
all in all it's a happy and peaceful image of domestic bliss.

SCENE TWO

ELISABETH *smells the white autumn asters.*

ELISABETH: What a long time they last. Five days already.
    When we first met I never imagined you'd buy me white
    asters.
POLICEMAN: Soon as I saw them, some inner voice.
ELISABETH: All the same.
POLICEMAN: What did you think, this dashing policeman's
    bound to be a fickle butterfly? On the lookout for a rich
    woman? Big mistake. Someone depends on me means
    much more to me than the other way round. What about
    another kiss?
ELISABETH: All right.
POLICEMAN: Is the coffee nearly ready?
ELISABETH: Any minute.
    (*The* POLICEMAN *takes some earphones from the bedside table*
    and puts them on.)
POLICEMAN: Attention! Very dashing . . .
    (*He hums along with the Radetzky March, which is being*
    played on the radio.)
ELISABETH: Listen, Alfons . . . last night there was a wonderful
    opera broadcast. *Aida.*

31

(*The* POLICEMAN *puts the earphones back on the bedside table.*)

POLICEMAN: Weren't you missing me?

ELISABETH: Alfons!

POLICEMAN: What about another kiss?

ELISABETH: Here's your coffee . . . (*She brings him a cup.*) And here's your kiss . . . (*She kisses him and sits on the edge of the bed. The* POLICEMAN *sips his coffee pleasurably.*)

POLICEMAN: Thank God we've got through to today. Constant state of emergency . . . good thing the bloody elections are over. Night before last another of my mates was shot.

ELISABETH: There's always been massacre of the innocents.

POLICEMAN: Wouldn't happen if we had law and order.

ELISABETH: I can see there's always been injustices, because of man's inhumanity to man . . . all you can hope for is a few less injustices.

POLICEMAN: Never mind the philosophy. What d'you like most about me?

ELISABETH: Everything.

POLICEMAN: But what word describes me best?

ELISABETH: I don't know.

POLICEMAN: Go on, you must know.

ELISABETH: You've changed a bit, Alfons. You used to be sadder.

POLICEMAN: What d'you mean?

ELISABETH: Well, more melancholy.

POLICEMAN: Oh, I still am. Don't make me laugh!

ELISABETH: I'm sorry . . .

(*She gets up.*)

POLICEMAN: Where are you going? Oh, I see. Don't wrap a corset round your feelings.

(ELISABETH *flinches, speaks sharply.*)

ELISABETH: What d'you mean, a corset?

POLICEMAN: (*Surprised*) Why?

(*Silence.* ELISABETH *smiles.*)

ELISABETH: I'm sorry, I'm a bit jumpy today . . .

(*She leaves the room.*)

SCENE THREE

POLICEMAN: (*Alone*) . . . melancholy? More melancholy? . . .
What d'you mean, more melancholy?

SCENE FOUR

ELISABETH *reappears.*

POLICEMAN: You've been a long time.
ELISABETH: Have I?
POLICEMAN: Nothing the matter, is there?
ELISABETH: I don't understand what you mean.
POLICEMAN: I've always been very careful.
ELISABETH: Oh, I see.

SCENE FIVE

*There's a knock on the door. The lovers listen . . . but there's
another knock, this time more decisive.*

POLICEMAN: Sh! No one at home.
ELISABETH: Who can it be?

SCENE SIX

VOICE: Police!
ELISABETH: Jesus Christ!
POLICEMAN: Police? And I'm stuck here. Yes, we have no
bananas!
(*He hurriedly gathers up his clothes and hides in the wardrobe.*)

33

The knocking at the door is even more decisive. ELISABETH *opens the door and a man steps into the bed-sitting room. He's a* CHIEF INSPECTOR *from the Vice Squad.*

CHIEF INSPECTOR: Everything comes to him who waits. (*He looks around and points to the unmade bed.*) I wake you up?

ELISABETH: Why?

CHIEF INSPECTOR: You know why.

ELISABETH: I'm not feeling at my best today.

CHIEF INSPECTOR: Now there are people who work all night, they tend to need a bit of a rest during the day.

ELISABETH: I don't know what you mean.

(*The* CHIEF INSPECTOR *flourishes a suspender, which he's found on the chair.*)

CHIEF INSPECTOR: Hold your socks up with suspenders, do you?

(*Silence.*)

ELISABETH: What d'you want?

CHIEF INSPECTOR: You received an employment order from the police, which states that within three weeks you would seek *certified* employment. But not only do you not have a job, there's no indication you've made any attempt to find one.

ELISABETH: Why don't you worry about the real unemployed?

CHIEF INSPECTOR: I didn't come here for a political diatribe. Being unemployed is not contrary to police regulations, what's contrary to police regulations is being a threat to public order.

ELISABETH: But I'm not a threat to public order.

CHIEF INSPECTOR: As long as you remain unable to give a satisfactory account of your earnings, that remains open to debate.

ELISABETH: I've been taken care of.

CHIEF INSPECTOR: Precisely and it is the nature of this care which we're interested in.

ELISABETH: But I've explained that already. My fiancé gives me twenty marks a week. That's what I live on.

CHIEF INSPECTOR: Who is he, this fiancé?

(*Silence.*)

Naming no names, is it?

ELISABETH: No.

CHIEF INSPECTOR: And why not?

ELISABETH: Because of his position, I wouldn't want to do him any harm.

CHIEF INSPECTOR: (*Grinning*) Nice! Very nice . . . are you sure there aren't several fiancés who club together for this twenty marks?

ELISABETH: How dare you . . .

CHIEF INSPECTOR: (*Interrupting her*) Now, calm down, miss, I'm sure you'll excuse me if I'm out of order . . .

(*Suddenly he opens the wardrobe and is unsurprised to find a man in it, although the fact this man is a policeman in underpants, wearing only the jacket and cap of his uniform, seems to cause him some embarrassment.*)

SCENE EIGHT

The POLICEMAN *stands to attention in the wardrobe.*

CHIEF INSPECTOR: You?

POLICEMAN: Everything she said is true, sir.

(*Silence.*)

CHIEF INSPECTOR: (*To* ELISABETH) Would you leave us for a moment? . . .

(ELISABETH *hesitates.*)

POLICEMAN: (*To* ELISABETH) Please.

ELISABETH: All right.

(*She exits.*)

35

CHIEF INSPECTOR: So this is where you spend your free time?
  (*The* POLICEMAN *has climbed out of the wardrobe and is now hurriedly dressing.*)
POLICEMAN: If you'd let me explain, sir . . . I'm sure there's been some mistake.
CHIEF INSPECTOR: Mistake? Where did you find this woman? We've got her under observation, we believe she belongs to a particular class of girl.
POLICEMAN: What class of girl?
CHIEF INSPECTOR: Use your imagination.
  (*Silence. The* POLICEMAN *smiles.*)
POLICEMAN: No, no, sir . . .
CHIEF INSPECTOR: How well d'you know her?
POLICEMAN: I know her.
CHIEF INSPECTOR: And you want to marry her?
POLICEMAN: I had it in mind, sir.
CHIEF INSPECTOR: How old are you?
POLICEMAN: Twenty-four. Sir.
CHIEF INSPECTOR: Same old story.
  (*The* POLICEMAN *has finished dressing.*)
POLICEMAN: But it's true what she says about the twenty marks, sir.
CHIEF INSPECTOR: Eighty marks a month! Are we overpaying you?
POLICEMAN: My parents help out.
CHIEF INSPECTOR: What's your father do?
POLICEMAN: Master carpenter.
CHIEF INSPECTOR: Perhaps you'd have done better to stick to woodwork.
POLICEMAN: I'm not sure I follow, sir.
  (*Silence.*)
CHIEF INSPECTOR: I'm sorry about this, but you don't seem to be aware who it is you're proposing to lead to the altar . . . your fiancée has done fourteen days in gaol for fraud.

POLICEMAN: Gaol?
CHIEF INSPECTOR: For fraud. Not to mention a fine she'd
    already been landed with. For that kind of woman I can
    understand a relationship with the police might be highly
    desirable. But I can't think it'd be very beneficial to your
    career . . .
POLICEMAN: I had no idea . . .
CHIEF INSPECTOR: Well, then. (*He opens the door and calls out.*)
    Come in!

SCENE TEN

ELISABETH *comes back in. She already knows it's all over. Silence.*

POLICEMAN: Fraud? Is that right?
ELISABETH: I know it's over.
POLICEMAN: Gaol?
ELISABETH: Yes.
    (*Silence.*)
POLICEMAN: Listen, Elisabeth. Why didn't you tell me?
ELISABETH: Don't ask bloody silly questions.
    (*Silence. The* POLICEMAN *stands to attention.*)
POLICEMAN: Thank you very much, sir!
CHIEF INSPECTOR: Not at all.
    (*The* POLICEMAN *clicks his heels and starts to leave.*)
ELISABETH: Wait!
    (*Silence.*)
POLICEMAN: You lied to me, that's the main thing.
ELISABETH: No, your career, that's the main thing for you.
POLICEMAN: It's not! But duty comes first and that's the way it
    will always be. Always!
    (*Silence.*)
ELISABETH: Oh, Alfons. Just now . . . when you were in the
    wardrobe I tried to protect you.
POLICEMAN: Me?
ELISABETH: Us.

37

POLICEMAN: Yourself! Yourself at my expense! I know what's
what!
(*Silence.* ELISABETH *grins.*)
ELISABETH: I didn't want to lose you, love . . .
(*The* POLICEMAN *clicks his heels again.*)
POLICEMAN: Sir!
(*He exits, fast.*)

SCENE ELEVEN

CHIEF INSPECTOR: That really wasn't necessary, you know, to
risk his career like that, most inconsiderate . . .
ELISABETH: Necessary? What about my career?
CHIEF INSPECTOR: You're not going to pretend you were
innocent?
ELISABETH: Oh, no, I gave that up a long time ago. I'm sorry, I
can't help laughing . . .
(*She sits on the edge of the bed, silent laughter.*)
CHIEF INSPECTOR: That's right, you have a good laugh.
(*He exits. Darkness.*)

ACT FIVE

SCENE ONE

Police station. After midnight.
The POLICEMAN (*Alfons Klostermeyer*) *is playing chess with a colleague. It's raining outside and far in the distance (until Scene Three) a band is playing Chopin's much loved Funeral March.*

SCENE TWO

The POLICEMAN *listens.*

POLICEMAN: Who's that playing?
SECOND POLICEMAN: The radio.
POLICEMAN: After midnight?
SECOND POLICEMAN: Maybe it's America. Still daytime there.
    It's your go.
POLICEMAN: Right.
    (*Pause. The* POLICEMAN *moves his rook. The* SECOND
    POLICEMAN *ponders.*)
SECOND POLICEMAN: If I go here, you'll go there. If I go there,
    you'll go here. One fine day in the middle of the night, two
    dead men got up to fight . . . Bishop to C3. Check.
POLICEMAN: So that's the way of it.
    (*Pause.*)
    Whose go is it?
SECOND POLICEMAN: Always the person who asks.
    (*Pause. The* POLICEMAN *gets up.*)
POLICEMAN: I give up. Mate.
SECOND POLICEMAN: Mate? With that board?
POLICEMAN: I'm stymied.
SECOND POLICEMAN: What about queen to D7? Or knight to
    G4?
POLICEMAN: Suppose so.

SCENE THREE

The SECOND POLICEMAN *is still looking at the chessboard.*

SECOND POLICEMAN: Not like you to throw in the towel, you usually hang on to the bitter end, even when the prospects are hopeless.

POLICEMAN: I'm not feeling well. For some time now. When I lie down I'm wide awake, when I get up I keep falling asleep.

SECOND POLICEMAN: It's your nerves.

POLICEMAN: (*Smiles painfully*) Yes, well, I've just had a bit of a shake up.

SECOND POLICEMAN: Professional?

POLICEMAN: No. Private. Woman trouble. You put yourself on the line and do everything for someone, support her and devote your deepest feelings, your free time and your good money to her . . . and what happens? She makes a monkey out of you.

SECOND POLICEMAN: Ingratitude how like a serpent's tooth.

POLICEMAN: So sometimes I can't help brooding.

SECOND POLICEMAN: You mustn't do that! Brooding's fatal!

POLICEMAN: I don't care. Look . . . take my first fiancée, I got on really well with her, she went and died on me. So that's it. One dies, the other's a liar. Nothing but bleeding disappointments. I can't find anyone whose love's got something in it for me.

SCENE FOUR

And now a THIRD POLICEMAN *comes into the station bringing with him the* DISSECTOR, *who's completely drunk . . . the* ASSISTANT DISSECTOR *is there as well, also a little the worse for wear from over-indulgence.*

THIRD POLICEMAN: Right. Here we are.

ASSISTANT DISSECTOR: Now look here, officer . . .

THIRD POLICEMAN: (*Interrupting him*) Quiet! (*To his colleagues*) Drunk and disorderly and disturbing the peace.

ASSISTANT DISSECTOR: How d'you get disturbing the peace?

THIRD POLICEMAN: How do I get it? Wasn't he ranting and raving and banging his walking stick against the shutters, waking the whole street up? And did he call me a moron and a pinhead? Or didn't he?
(*Silence.*)

ASSISTANT DISSECTOR: I'm sorry, originally all we intended was a modest celebration of this gentleman's sixty-second birthday, but man proposes . . .

SECOND POLICEMAN: (*Grinning*) . . . and God disposes.

DISSECTOR: (*Shrilly*) And who's to blame? The Chief Dissector.

THIRD POLICEMAN: Quiet! (*He points to the chessboard.*) Who won?

SECOND POLICEMAN: Me.

THIRD POLICEMAN: You? Beat him? Impossible.

POLICEMAN: I'm not in the mood.

DISSECTOR: Gentlemen! Who is my enemy? The Chief Dissector and only the Chief Dissector.

THIRD POLICEMAN: Will you put a sock in it!

SECOND POLICEMAN: Why's he keep going on about this Chief Dissector?

ASSISTANT DISSECTOR: Actually he is the Chief Dissector . . . I'm an Assistant Dissector and this gentleman here is my Chief. He was promoted last month, but when he's drunk, he always forgets about the promotion. The Chief Dissector the Chief Dissector here is talking about kicked the bucket some time ago, thank God . . . he got an infection off a corpse. From Brno.

THIRD POLICEMAN: Will you shut up! Sit down! Give me the charge book!

SCENE FIVE

The BOOK-KEEPER *bursts in.*

BOOK-KEEPER: Help, officer! There's a woman in the canal!
POLICEMAN: In the canal?
THIRD POLICEMAN: What woman?
BOOK-KEEPER: A suicide! We pulled her out of the water . . .
    that's to say, not me, but this daring young lifesaver. I
    think she's still alive! Here they are!

SCENE SIX

*Two men, one in a dinner-jacket, appear and with them the daring
young lifesaver,* JOACHIM. *They're carrying* ELISABETH, *who's
been rescued from the canal. They lay her down on a bench.*
JOACHIM *is completely soaked and frozen through . . . a*
POLICEMAN *hands him a blanket, which he wraps round himself.
Everyone, except for the* DISSECTOR, *now busies himself with*
ELISABETH. *The* POLICEMAN, *Alfons Klostermeyer, also steps up
to her, recognizes her and stares at her.*

BOOK-KEEPER: There's still a spark of life in her . . .
THIRD POLICEMAN: Artificial respiration right away!
ASSISTANT DISSECTOR: I know how to do that. May I be of
    assistance? I did two terms as a medical student but then
    the money ran out and . . .
SECOND POLICEMAN: Get on with it!
DISSECTOR: And what about some schnapps?
JOACHIM: Yes, I'd like some too.
DISSECTOR: (*To* JOACHIM) Real guts. Pitch-black night
    in November, jumping in the water . . . daring! Very
    daring!
JOACHIM: I was only doing my natural human duty.
    (*He drinks from the schnapps bottle.*)

DISSECTOR: Too modest, you're too modest!
  (*He takes the schnapps bottle from him and turns to the*
  POLICEMAN.)
  Isn't that right, general?
POLICEMAN: I'm not a general.
DISSECTOR: Well, here's to the daring young lifesaver! Cheers!
  (*He drinks.*)
JOACHIM: (*To the* POLICEMAN) I was walking past and I heard
  this splash and then I saw a sort of silvery glow . . . that
  was her face. So I jumped straight in and grabbed her.
  Matter of honour. Anybody would have done it. You
  would.
POLICEMAN: Of course.
DISSECTOR: It'll look good in the papers. With a photograph.
  Long live the daring young lifesaver! Cheers!
  (*He drinks again. The* THIRD POLICEMAN *is with*
  ELISABETH.)
THIRD POLICEMAN: Where's that schnapps?
DISSECTOR: Here!
JOACHIM: (*To the* POLICEMAN) Can I use the telephone?
POLICEMAN: Over there.
  (*The* SECOND POLICEMAN *comes up to the* POLICEMAN.)
SECOND POLICEMAN: She had nothing on her. Except an out-
  of-date sales permit.
DISSECTOR: Sales permit?
SECOND POLICEMAN: That's right.
  (*The* DISSECTOR *turns to* ELISABETH *and looks at her
  closely.*)

SCENE SEVEN

While everybody, except for the POLICEMAN *and the two men, who
have already left the police station, is busy with* ELISABETH
(*administering artificial respiration and so on*), *including the*
DISSECTOR, JOACHIM *telephones his mum.*

43

JOACHIM: Hello, Mum! Is that you, Mum? . . . No, don't worry, I didn't mean to wake you up, but I've just saved someone's life, a girl who was trying to kill herself . . . Daring, eh? Well, it was a matter of honour. It'll be in the papers, with a photograph, how's that for a priceless ad for the firm, in all the papers for nothing . . . Hello! So do I get my motor-bike now? . . . What? But you promised! We'll see? Goodbye! (*He hangs up, furious. To himself*) Silly old cow.

SCENE EIGHT

POLICEMAN: Is she dead?
SECOND POLICEMAN: I think she's breathing.
ASSISTANT DISSECTOR: We'll see. We'll see.

SCENE NINE

The DISSECTOR *has recognized* ELISABETH.

DISSECTOR: That's her. No question. The one who . . . (*He turns to the* POLICEMAN, *repentant.*) Your honour . . .
POLICEMAN: (*Interrupting him*) Leave me alone!
DISSECTOR: You must listen to me, please . . . I have a confession to make. That woman has been murdered.
POLICEMAN: (*Startled*) Murdered?
DISSECTOR: I know the murderer.
POLICEMAN: What are you talking about?
(*Silence.*)
DISSECTOR: The whole business with the government inspector and the claims inspector . . . it was all my fault, m'lud! An eye for an eye, a tooth for a tooth! Take me away and get it over with! Do me a favour, hang me high!
ASSISTANT DISSECTOR: (*To the* POLICEMAN) He gets pangs of conscience.

44

POLICEMAN: (*To the* DISSECTOR) You pig!
DISSECTOR: Oh, God! (*He sits down in a corner.*) I'll be calm and
    collected on the scaffold . . . do your duty, hangman! And
    pray for me, good people, may you not be led into
    temptation, and before you do anything you might regret,
    remember me . . .
    (*He buries his face in his hands and sits there shaking.*)

SCENE TEN

THIRD POLICEMAN: She's coming to!

SCENE ELEVEN

ELISABETH *regains consciousness, but she's still not quite there . . .
she sits up on the bench and looks around. She still doesn't grasp
what's going on and remembers only gradually.*

SCENE TWELVE

ELISABETH: (*To the* BOOK-KEEPER) Who are you?
BOOK-KEEPER: Who, me?
    (*Silence. The* THIRD POLICEMAN *passes her the schnapps
    bottle.*)
THIRD POLICEMAN: There you are, miss . . .
    (ELISABETH *is still staring at the* BOOK-KEEPER.)
ELISABETH: Who are you?
ASSISTANT DISSECTOR: (*To the* BOOK-KEEPER) Go on, tell her!
BOOK-KEEPER: Me? Nobody . . .
ELISABETH: (*Smiling*) Nobody . . . (*Suddenly she looks around,
    frightened.*) Am I still alive?
SECOND POLICEMAN: (*Smiling*) Course you are.
    (*The* THIRD POLICEMAN *is still holding out the schnapps
    bottle for her.*)

45

THIRD POLICEMAN: There you are, miss . . .

(ELISABETH *is suddenly staring at the* SECOND POLICEMAN, *terrified*.)

ELISABETH: What's that you're wearing?

SECOND POLICEMAN: (*Somewhat confused*) What do you mean?

ELISABETH: Green and grey and silver . . . have you got me again? Now what have I done wrong?

THIRD POLICEMAN: Just calm down. We're here to protect you. Don't worry.

ELISABETH: (*Absently*) Who was it breathed on me?

SECOND POLICEMAN: Just come back down to earth, miss . . . listen, you only live once, you don't want to go throwing yourself in the water.

ELISABETH: Was it you fished me out?

JOACHIM: Me.

(*Silence*.)

ELISABETH: Why couldn't you mind your own business?

JOACHIM: Oh, very nice.

ELISABETH: I'd got away and now it's all starting again, when no one's responsible for you and life is meaningless . . .

(*The* ASSISTANT DISSECTOR *touches her shoulder*.)

ASSISTANT DISSECTOR: You mustn't give up hope . . . everyone's life has a meaning, if not for them then for somebody else.

ELISABETH: Not mine.

ASSISTANT DISSECTOR: Yes!

ELISABETH: No!

ASSISTANT DISSECTOR: (*To the* SECOND POLICEMAN) I can get really annoyed when I'm contradicted. I work with corpses on a daily basis and your thoughts automatically turn to the meaning of life. In my experience as an Assistant Dissector . . .

ELISABETH: (*Interrupting him*) An Assistant Dissector? . . . (*Shrilly*) How's the good old Dissector? Still feeding the pigeons?

SCENE THIRTEEN

DISSECTOR: Absolutely! (*He rises to his feet, full of dignity, if still a little unsteady.*) Those pigeons sit on my shoulder and eat out of my hand, my canary sings and I have a trained snake. I have a cage full of white mice and my three goldfish are called Anton, Josef and Herbert. I must demand, I must emphatically demand your attention. You don't seem to be aware who I am! I am the Chief Dissector, after all. And if I feel like killing someone that's a matter between me and my conscience. To sort out face to face with God! All right, officer! Good morning, all!
(*He exits. Everyone except* ELISABETH *involuntarily clicks his heels.*)

ALL: Good morning, sir!

SCENE FOURTEEN

ELISABETH *catches sight of her* POLICEMAN, *starts up and bites her hand.*

ASSISTANT DISSECTOR: Now now!
(*Silence.*)

BOOK-KEEPER: I think she's hallucinating.

JOACHIM: It's no joke, you know, freezing-cold water this time of year on a pitch-black night.
(ELISABETH *slowly covers her eyes with her hand, as if she were blinded by the sun.*)

ELISABETH: Is that you, Alfons?
(*Silence.*)

SECOND POLICEMAN: What's the matter, Klostermeyer? Do you know each other?

ELISABETH: Do we know each other?
(*Silence.*)
Go on, tell them if you know me . . .

47

POLICEMAN: We know each other.

ELISABETH: (*Grinning*) Good, very good . . .

(*Silence.*)

How's your career?

THIRD POLICEMAN: (*To* ALFONS KLOSTERMEYER) What's all this about?

POLICEMAN: Later.

ELISABETH: Why not now?

(*Silence. The* POLICEMAN *pulls on his white gloves.*)

POLICEMAN: I have to go. I'm on guard duty.

ELISABETH: Guard duty?

POLICEMAN: In front of the palace. At dawn.

ELISABETH: It's still dark, Alfons.

POLICEMAN: Everything's settled between us.

ELISABETH: You think so?

POLICEMAN: It's over.

(*Silence.*)

ELISABETH: How simple you make it sound . . .

POLICEMAN: Don't say any more, please.

ELISABETH: (*Smiles maliciously*) Why not?

(*Silence.*)

POLICEMAN: Don't try and start an argument for no reason. How can I help it if, if you want to throw yourself in the water? I stretched out my hand to you . . .

ELISABETH: (*Interrupting him*) Pity you didn't cut it off!

(*Silence.*)

I'm going now . . . can you hear me, Alfons?

(*The* THIRD POLICEMAN *blocks her exit.*)

THIRD POLICEMAN: Stop!

(ELISABETH *looks straight at him.*)

ELISABETH: Good night.

THIRD POLICEMAN: No.

(*Silence.*)

ELISABETH: Just let me go . . .

THIRD POLICEMAN: Where?

ELISABETH: None of your business.

THIRD POLICEMAN: Under the circumstances we're keeping you here. It's our duty.

(*Silence. Once again* ELISABETH *smiles maliciously.*)

ELISABETH: Are you taking me in again?

SECOND POLICEMAN: Not into custody. Only into protective custody.

ELISABETH: Locking me up?

THIRD POLICEMAN: In your own interests.

ELISABETH: Funny. Here you all are, standing around, stopping people getting their sales permits . . .

(*She grins.*)

ASSISTANT DISSECTOR: Now, don't be childish . . .

ELISABETH: I'm not speaking personally, I don't give a damn about that any more . . . (*Suddenly she yells at* ALFONS.) Stop staring at me like that! Get out of my sight or I'll pull my eyes out! And don't imagine I threw myself in because of you, you with the big future! I threw myself in the water because I had nothing to eat . . . if I'd had something to eat do you think I'd have even bothered to spit in your eye? Don't look at me like that! (*She throws the schnapps bottle at his eyes, but misses.*) There!

(*The* SECOND POLICEMAN *grabs hold of her arm.*)

SECOND POLICEMAN: Stop that!

ELISABETH: Let go!

JOACHIM: No, don't!

ELISABETH: (*Yelling*) Let go! Let go!

THIRD POLICEMAN: Quiet!

JOACHIM: Ow! She bit me!

ASSISTANT DISSECTOR: What's that? Biting are you . . . biting?

(ELISABETH *cowers, intimidated.*)

BOOK-KEEPER: Biting the man who saved her life . . .

(ELISABETH *snarls, baring her teeth.*)

SCENE FIFTEEN

A band marches by in the distance, playing the march 'Alte Kameraden'. Then the music fades and ELISABETH *sits slumped in a chair.*

SCENE SIXTEEN

POLICEMAN: Guard duty . . . (*He puts on his helmet.*) Mustn't be late.

SECOND POLICEMAN: There's time, Klostermeyer. Wait for us . . .
(*He pulls on his white gloves.*)

THIRD POLICEMAN: We have to go too.

ASSISTANT DISSECTOR: What's that rumbling noise?

BOOK-KEEPER: This lady's stomach.

THIRD POLICEMAN: (*To the* SECOND POLICEMAN) Have you got something?

SECOND POLICEMAN: Sure . . .
(*He hands* ELISABETH *a roll out of his coat pocket.*
ELISABETH *takes it apathetically and gnaws at it. The* THIRD POLICEMAN *pulls on his white gloves.*)

THIRD POLICEMAN: Nice?
(ELISABETH *smiles apathetically . . . suddenly she drops the roll and collapses across the table.*)

ASSISTANT DISSECTOR: Whoops!

THIRD POLICEMAN: Now!
(*He and the* ASSISTANT DISSECTOR *busy themselves with* ELISABETH.)

SECOND POLICEMAN: Just fainted.

BOOK-KEEPER: Probably her stomach . . .

ASSISTANT DISSECTOR: A weak heart.

BOOK-KEEPER: Stomach or heart, sheep or a lamb.

JOACHIM: It's no joke, you know, on a pitch-black night in November in freezing-cold water . . .

ASSISTANT DISSECTOR: (*To* ELISABETH) There we are, there we are . . .
  (ELISABETH *comes to and smiles weakly.*)
ELISABETH: Can I see someone in authority?
THIRD POLICEMAN: In authority?
ELISABETH: (*Nods*) It's quite urgent . . . it'll be worse before
  it's better, but I never let it get me down . . . (*She waves
  her hand in the air, as if she were trying to fend off flies.*) Ah,
  it's these kind of black worms flying around . . .
  (*She dies gently.*)

SCENE SEVENTEEN

The BOOK-KEEPER *quietly approaches the dead* ELISABETH *and
knocks on the table-top.*

BOOK-KEEPER: (*Cautiously*) Come in, miss. Your time is up!
THIRD POLICEMAN: I fear the worst.
  (*The* POLICEMAN *takes off his helmet. The* ASSISTANT
  DISSECTOR *bends over* ELISABETH.)
ASSISTANT DISSECTOR: She's passed away. Heart most likely.
  We'll have a look tomorrow . . .
JOACHIM: All for nothing . . .
  (*He exits.*)

SCENE EIGHTEEN

POLICEMAN: For nothing . . . (*He crosses to his dead* ELISABETH
  and strokes her hair.) Poor love. Just my luck. Just my luck.
BOOK-KEEPER: I'm alive, but how long for?
  I don't know when I'll die.
  I don't know where I'm headed for.
  I'm happy: wonder why?
  (*He exits.*)

SCENE NINETEEN

ASSISTANT DISSECTOR: A poet.
THIRD POLICEMAN: Still raining.
SECOND POLICEMAN: The parade'll be rained off.
POLICEMAN: Probably.
ASSISTANT DISSECTOR: Well, I'll say goodbye . . .
  (*He exits.*)

SCENE TWENTY

And now a band marches by outside . . . once again playing the march 'Alte Kameraden'. The three policemen put their helmets on and leave the station, because, as you know, they're on guard duty. Only ALFONS KLOSTERMEYER *sneaks a last look at his dead fiancée,* ELISABETH.